EYES TO SEE

NORA V. BORDT

WestBow Press books may be ordered through booksellers or by contacting:

WestBow Press
A Division of Thomas Nelson & Zondervan
1663 Liberty Drive
Bloomington, IN 47403
www.westbowpress.com
844-714-3454

Scripture quotations taken from The Holy Bible, New International Version® NIV® Copyright © 1973 1978 1984 2011 by Biblica, Inc. TM. Used by permission. All rights reserved worldwide.

ISBN: 978-1-6642-2167-3 (sc)
ISBN: 978-1-6642-2166-6 (hc)
ISBN: 978-1-6642-2168-0 (e)

Library of Congress Control Number: 2021901890

Print information available on the last page.

WestBow Press rev. date: 03/03/2021

WESTBOW
PRESS®
A DIVISION OF THOMAS NELSON
& ZONDERVAN

INTRODUCTION

Ears to hear
—Matthew 11:15

Whoever has ears, let him hear what the Spirit says to the churches.
—Revelation 2:29

The Lord gifted me with a love for His creation at a very early age. I can remember lying in the snow (I love the snow, by the way) in our backyard in upstate New York. I remember how the sun looked and how the snow felt around me. Most of all, I noticed the sparkle in the snow and the brilliant sunshine, and I was in love! And although I knew about the Lord, during those times, I realized He was showing His love for me.

So what can I say except my heart continues to marvel at creation? And my heart desires to share this love in hopes of inspiring faith in the Lord Jesus Christ and a desire to extend this love to others.

I invite you to go with me to these beautiful examples of creation.

This book contains my paintings of beautiful places in creation that the Lord has blessed me and my family to see and photograph.

May the Lord bless us all with *eyes to see.*

Lord, I thank You for the abundance of beauty in Your creation. The cool air rising up the mountain is soothing for my soul. Where else could we go, Lord, to get such a refreshing? You have such abundance for us, Lord, and the more we take in this view, the more we sense Your presence with us. The light is so brilliant up here, Lord. But I know, Lord, that the valley is part of Your creation also. It is here where we "see" You in a different way. Where our hearts open through pain or disappointment. But then we find that You are there just the same. The contrasting dullness of the light allows our hearts to focus on You. You have this "valley situation," Lord, and I know You have me.

Wow, Lord. When we look at the strength of this tree, we wonder how many storms it has weathered. How much wind, snow, ice, and drought has it flourished in? We see that You created it to thrive. Thank You, Lord, for creating us to thrive as long as we are rooted in You!

And the beauty of these mountains! They gleam and glow in all changing seasons. The colors fill up our hearts with joy!

We see that You are the Mighty Lord who is steadfast and unchanging in every season. And we see that You provide strength for us to flourish in You.

Give us eyes to see, Lord.

Nora Bordt © 2020

Lord, I thank You for the light. It bounces off the mountains, illuminates the sky, shines translucently through the waves, and splashes exuberantly over the rocks. What a blessing that You have provided these glorious light shows for us. So wonderful to see, Lord.

Thank You that You cause truth to shine for us, Lord! All we have to do is be willing to open our eyes to what You have for us. Sometimes Your truth is spread abroad over the vast mountains, shining brightly in the distance and leading us on. Sometimes Your truth illuminates the whole sky and fills our hearts with assurance that it is truly You who are leading. Sometimes Your truth shines through and brightens up an area where darkness had hidden the way. Oh, how we thank You for that clarity, Lord.

Thank You, Lord, that when we are most in need, Your truth splashes on our situation like the light illuminating the crashing waves! How unexpected and startling it is, Lord! It surprises and shakes us, and we end up thanking You for whatever change that truth called for. You always know the right time, the right place, and the right direction we need to stay in the light of Your truth.

Give us eyes to see, Lord.

John 1:17
Psalm 143:8

There are going to be days like this. Not a particularly pretty sky, chilling wind, and dangerous rocks.

Yet there are spiritual treasures all around. The sun is still shining beautifully, just beyond the cloud level. Everything that tries to hide the joy of Your love cannot negate it. Your love still shines.

Those rocks look treacherous, hard, and imposing, yet imperceptibly the power of each wave break softens the sharp edges over time.

"Over time" is a phrase we don't really want to hear. "But Lord," we say, "why not now? Why not here?" Those waves are not going anywhere, no matter how strong the jagged rocks seem. Your everlasting love and power do not change, and what was brought against us will have to submit to Him.

We can see the trees mounted like trophies on the edge of this crashing sea. They stand tall against all that icy wind with roots that find spaces to anchor on. Oh Lord, thank You for providing spaces for us to anchor our faith into. You knew what each of us individually would face in this life, and Your provision gives us courage and joy.

Thank You, Lord, for providing a horizon for us to rest our gaze on. The light out there is brighter and hints of joys to come. Give us eyes to see, Lord.

Lamentations 3:22
Psalm 28:7

Nora Bordi © 2020

Oh Lord, how wonderful it is when You fill our hearts with anticipation! We see what is ahead, gleaming in the summer sunlight like the enticing water below! We know there is a beach and a shore full of delights.

Father, You have laid before us an overwhelmingly precious future with You and earthly delights to fill us with the joy of knowing You here until eternity comes.

This path to this beautiful beach is hidden from where we are standing, and we wonder how the descent will be. Will it be steep, rocky, and hidden in the tangle of seaside foliage? How long will it take us? Who is going to help us find the path? Will we be able to carry everything? Or will it be cool and enticing as we make our way down? Will the joy of anticipation carry us in seemingly no time at all? You know, Lord.

Either way, Lord, we thank You as we journey with You through our days. Give us eyes to see, Lord.

Nora Bordt © 2020

Lord, we often say that we want to see what is at the farthest reaches of those mountains. What events are happening there? Will it be very different from here? Will we know what to do? Will we know what to say? It is so far away that nothing is clear. There are no details to see. We can imagine that it will be similar to the area we can see closer up. Maybe the trees will be the same; maybe the situation will be the same. We really wonder about those places in our lives and situations that are way far in the distance.

And then we hear You speaking to our hearts. And we can sense Your sweet invitation to rest awhile with You on this wall, to allow You time to refresh our hearts with the beauty You created.

We struggle with that sometimes, and those questions about that far-off distance really grow strong and resist what the Lord just asked us to do.

Lord, let us desire to see You more than we desire to see what's in the distance. After all, we should really remind ourselves that You have already been down there. You know what's there. But while we worry about what we know, You are more concerned about how we see, both ourselves and You.

Give us eyes to see, Lord. That's what we really need.

We love seeing the sun on the water, Lord. It sparkles, it dances, and it makes the day so happy to our hearts. We love the waves crashing against the sand. They bring us consistency. We know after one wave crashes and rolls back to the sea that another wave is right behind it.

How that is like life in You, Lord. We know that You are consistent in all that You do. That brings such comfort to our hearts and gives us courage as we face things that seem out of control. We know that You are in control and that just like the waves, there will be a consistency in You. You will always be there for us. You always have a word for our heart if we take time to listen. You always affirm Your love for us by Your creation. You always stay with us until the waves resolve and the next one comes.

Thank You, Lord, for our being able to trust You that way. Please grow us into Your children who are more consistent in our trust in You and our love for You, in inner joy in our relationship with You, and in our desire to show others who You are and who You want to be in our lives as our Father, Savior, and Holy Spirit.

We marvel, Lord, at the way the beautiful shorebirds skim, fly, and find their way through the crashing waves. You have made them excellent in their ability to change direction, to change speed, and to adapt their flight to catch their food. It looks so effortless to us, Lord.

Thank You, Lord, that as we allow You to sustain us, we also are able to change direction and our speed so that we can be where You need us to be, physically and spiritually. Where we can feed on Your Word, on the circumstance You want us to learn from, on the people You want us to listen to. Thank You, Lord, for making us flexible that way, and forgive us, Lord, when we insist on going our own way and not receiving direction from You to turn, slow down, speed up, or look in a new direction for what You have for us next. We want to be, and we need to be, dependent on You for those changes, and we know that we can trust You to lead us. We remember the word that You told the disciples that You didn't need any food the day You talked to the Samaritan John 4:1-25. You said Your food was doing Your will. Oh Father, how doing Your will satisfies.

(reference for well story)

Nora Bordt © 2020

Oh Father, how Your beautiful light reflects, if we will just have eyes to see! Even over stormy water when the sun breaks through the clouds, the brilliant light reflects off the water and makes it even more brilliant. We are sorry, Lord, for the times we complain when the clouds are dark and we find ourselves complaining, "Where is the light? Where is the light, Lord?" And then it happens! You break through with Your light—Your light of understanding, Your light of peace, Your light of grace, and Your light of love—and suddenly we see the darkness differently because of contrast with Your brilliant light.

Father, we pray that we shine like that for other people. We pray that when everything looks dark, You enable us to bring Your light. That You enable people to see how brilliantly You shine, especially in the darkness. Father, You bring the light of Your love through us. How precious and amazing that is. Father, forgive us when we don't carry that light when we complain instead of realizing what we have in Your light.

Father, we pray that so many others would know and be able to carry Your light with them to others who still in the darkness. What a blessing, Lord, to be able to discern by Your Spirit between the dark and the light.

It dazzles us to see that light shining off those dark waves piercing through the dark clouds. It makes us stop and realize the wonder of Your creation. Thank You, Lord, for giving us eyes to see.

Nora Bordt © 2020

How we marvel, Lord, in Your creation with every little detail. This includes the way the wind catches the little waves out in the middle of the bay, yet by the shore, the waves are calm. And we know, Father, that You have created different environments for different creatures. Some of the creatures need calm at the shore, and some of the creatures need the rough and tumble wild water to thrive.

We know, Father, that if You can create that special environment for each one of Your creatures, You take care of the environment that each one of us lives in. You have equipped us and provided for us to carry out Your will in these places, Lord, some of us in the quiet eddies by the shore. That's where we flourish, Lord. That is where we get to use the gifts that You have given us.

We know, Father, that You fit us, but oh how You made us! Our personalities and our emotions all fit with where You ask us to minister to others. Some flourish in the rough and tumble wide-open sea where the waves are so variable and the water runs so deep. You know the hearts that need that environment, and You know, Father, who are far from You in that environment. Thank You, Father, for that wonderful provision, for those wonderful details, and for the promise of Your presence in both the eddies and the calm waters as well as in the wild waves and the deep.

We love You, Lord! We desire to love You more and more as we look into the way Your creation mirrors the creation of our very lives.

What a beautiful place to stop and be with You, Lord! What a beautiful time in our lives, Lord, when You let us experience how peaceful Your creation can be. Beautiful sunshine streaming in and warming up the atmosphere, making the colors shine and dance. The sound of water dancing in the fountain and the brilliance of the individual droplets catch our attention. But Father, we know we can't order these peaceful times in our lives. We can't make this happen all the time. We can't live in this spot all the time. We know that for our good, Father, and for Your kingdom. We pray Your will be done, Father. We pray that Your kingdom would rule into our lives through any and every situation, including illness, unhappiness, trauma, grief, or chaos. Let Your kingdom come through any of those things, Father.

We know that You use everything, Lord, not just these beautiful calm times when we get to soak in the beauty of Your creation but also the trying times. We know that You are with us, and we know that nothing is wasted. We trust You, Lord. Give us eyes to see.

Nora Bordt © 2020

Printed in the United States
By Bookmasters